P9-BIE-761

ROCKIES

Carole Harmon Stephen Hutchings

Altitude Publishing

previous overleaf: *Snow Dome*, Columbia Icefield,
Jasper National Park, Don Harmon

ROCKIES

©Copyright, Altitude Publishing Ltd. All rights reserved.
English editions: 1982, 1983, 1985, 1987, 1989
ISBN 0-919381-05-7

Created, designed and produced in Canada.
Printed and bound in Japan.

Also available in: French ISBN 0-919381-40-5
                   German ISBN 0-919381-42-1
                   Japanese ISBN 0-919381-44-8

We gratefully acknowledge the assistance of the Alberta Foundation for the Literary Arts in the production of this book.

A streak of sunlight pierces the clouds to highlight Cathedral Mountain,
Yoho National Park, Stephen Hutchings

For a catalogue of Altitude titles, please write to:
Altitude Publishing Ltd.,
Box 490, Banff, Alberta, Canada
T0L 0C0
Telephone (403) 762-4548

cover: *Double rainbow, Castle Mountain*, Banff
National Park, Carole Harmon

ROCKIES
AN INTRODUCTION

The mountain environment of the Canadian Rockies is overwhelming and disquieting. It is hard to get a sense of direction, distance or scale. The skyline is broken with the jagged rhythms of mountain tops; the lower slopes are a profusion of detail; water seems to run everywhere. How can anyone make sense out of an environment so immense, so visually rich?

This state of confusion is not limited to the casual observer. It is shared by those who live and work in the mountains. It is definitely the case for those who wish to photograph them. The camera and the eye have a lot in common in this regard. It is very difficult to focus one's attention, let alone a camera lens, on any particular aspect of the mountains for more than a moment. Not only can we be distracted by the never-ending barrage of mountain detail, but our attention is also prey to the vagaries of light and weather that create a constant shift of emphasis.

There are some places in the Rockies that stand out from the rest–places such as Castle Mountain, Lake Louise, Athabasca Glacier, Mt. Edith Cavell, and Mt. Robson. They are distinctive in their own right and many of them have been the source of attention since man first came to the mountains. Mt. Edith Cavell, known to the voyageurs as La Montagne de la Grande Traverse, was used as a reference point for journeys over Athabasca Pass. Lake Louise was known to the Indians as the Lake of the Little Fishes that lay beneath the Great Snow Mountain. These places continue to exert their appeal over us. Hours, days and years have been spent studying, exploring, painting and photographing them. Walter Wilcox, one of the Rockies earliest photographers, told the following story about his photograph of Lake O'Hara: "It took me just four years to get that one. I believe I brought the camera back at least ten times, and when I finally had a promising day, I waited from eight till twelve o'clock for the psychological moment that brought the light I wanted on the water and the mountains."

Once we are at ease with the appearance and location of some of these familiar landmarks, we can venture forth to place them in a larger context, one which was initially a source of confusion. It is at this point that hikes into the backcountry can take on a greater significance. An experience on the trail that leads to Mt. Robson's north face illustrates this. The "standard view" of this famous mountain,

Glacier ice, Saskatchewan Glacier, Columbia Icefield, Banff National Park, Stephen Hutchings

the highest in the Canadian Rockies, is from the observation point located adjacent to the highway. Here, thousands of people each year derive their impressions of Mt. Robson. It is a familiar image. The trail, however, leads away from this into the dense valley forest of spruce, hemlock, cedar and Douglas fir. From the depths of the woods, the mountain cannot be seen. Only after we reach Kinney Lake, four kilometres distant, does it reappear. But is it Robson? The peak has so utterly transformed in appearance that only its location assures us that it is, indeed, the same mountain we gazed at from the road. A similar double-take occurs in another ten kilometres at Emperor Falls. And again at Berg Lake. Standing on the shore of the lake, we now look at the back side of the "standard view" of Robson. What was once familiar is now completely foreign. In the space of a few kilometres we have entered a new environment. Robson will never be the same again.

Similar revelations of form and feature occur whenever we probe behind the facade of the popular view. Around us, details abound. The patterns and relationships of a myriad of textures, plants, animals, rock and water link the whole together. The microcosm reveals the macrocosm. Rock walls twist and buckle in frozen testiment to the forces that formed the great mountains. Waterfalls thunder down from glaciers, cutting through the surface layers of rock to create new channels. Trees, plants and animals form a chain of existence which colours our every approach to the mountain environment. The brilliant yellow of a Glacier Lily, the delicate movement of Rocky Mountain sheep upon a slope, the crash of water over a steep cliff–details such as these transform the basis of our experience of the Rockies.

We begin to sense the inter-relationship of all these elements. The individual landmarks fit into the broad scenic views; the single details merge to form a pattern that, in turn, modifies the whole. And over all of this play the change of seasons and the constant shift of light and weather that make the same scene, observed or photographed at different times of day and year, appear as different, one from another, as if they were separate places altogether.

Stephen Hutchings

overleaf: *Wonder Pass*, Mt. Assiniboine Provincial Park, Carole Harmon

Mt. Robson, Mt. Robson Provincial Park, Carole Harmon

Mt. Robson and Berg Lake, Mt. Robson Provincial Park, Shin Sugino

opposite: *Wiwaxy Peak*, Yoho National Park, Carole Harmon

Lyall's Larch in autumn, Panorama Ridge, Banff National Park, Carole Harmon

opposite: *Bridal Veil Falls*, Banff National Park, Carole Harmon

Glacier Lilies, Carole Harmon

overleaf: *Springtime, Sunshine Meadows*, Avalanche Lilies and Western Anemone,
Banff National Park, Carole Harmon

Dolomite Peak, Banff National Park, Carole Harmon

North Canoe and South Canoe Glaciers, Cariboo Mountains, British Columbia, Carole Harmon

overleaf: *Mountain goat on Parkers Ridge*, Banff National Park, Don Harmon

Coyote, Shin Sugino

opposite: *Full moon through clouds*, Shin Sugino

Rearguard Falls, British Columbia, Carole Harmon

Reflections on Lake O'Hara, Yoho National Park, Carole Harmon

overleaf: *Moraine Lake*, Banff National Park, Don Harmon

Rappelling on Mt. Fryatt, Jasper National Park, Aileen Harmon

Climbers on the summit of Mt. Louis, Banff National Park, Stephen Hutchings

opposite: *Mt. Andromeda*, Columbia Icefield, Jasper National Park, Carole Harmon

U-shaped valley below Mt. Saskatchewan, Icefield Parkway, Banff National Park, Carole Harmon

overleaf: *Horsetail Ferns*, Stephen Hutchings

opposite: *Bighorn Sheep*, Rick Kunelius

On the Skyline Trail, Jasper National Park, Carole Harmon

overleaf: *Moss Campion*, Stephen Hutchings

Yellow Orchids, Carole Harmon

opposite: *Mt. Ringrose and Mt. Hungabee with the outlet stream of Lake Lefroy,* Yoho National Park, Carole Harmon

previous overleaf: *Rain on gooseberry leaves*, Carole Harmon

Sunrise on the Front Ranges, Jasper National Park, Shin Sugino

opposite: *Twin Falls*, Yoho National Park, Carole Harmon
overleaf: *Mt. Bergne*, the Freshfields, Banff National Park, Stephen Hutchings

opposite: *Mt. Lefroy and Lake Louise*, Banff National Park, Carole Harmon

Bow Lake, Banff National Park, Carole Harmon

overleaf: *Athabasca Glacier from Wilcox Pass*, Columbia Icefield, Jasper National Park, Carole Harmon

previous overleaf: *Crowfoot Glacier*, Banff National Park, Carole Harmon

Peyto Lake, Banff National Park, Don Harmon

opposite: *Mt. Edith Cavell*, Jasper National Park, Don Harmon

opposite: *Glacier on Mt. Athabasca*, Columbia Icefield, Jasper National Park, Carole Harmon

Winter reflections on Forty Mile Creek, Banff National Park, Aileen Harmon

overleaf: *Castle Mountain*, Banff National Park, Don Harmon

Ice cave, Saskatchewan Glacier, Columbia Icefield, Banff National Park, Carole Harmon

Catamount Glacier, Purcell Mountains, British Columbia, Aileen Harmon

On the trail to Grizzly Lake, Banff National Park, Carole Harmon

Approaching storm, Grizzly Lake, Banff National Park, Carole Harmon

overleaf: *The Freshfield Group from Niverville Meadows,* from left: Mt. Nanga Parbat, Mt. Walker, Prior Peak, and Mt. Pilkington, Banff National Park, Carole Harmon

Low lying clouds, Sunshine Meadows, Banff National Park, Carole Harmon

opposite: *Sunwapta Falls*, Jasper National Park, Stephen Hutchings

opposite: *Emperor Falls and Mt. Robson*, Mt. Robson Provincial Park, Aileen Harmon

Cummins Waterfall, Clemenceau Icefield, British Columbia, Aileen Harmon

Mt. Athabasca and Athabasca Glacier from Wilcox Pass, Jasper National Park, Stephen Hutchings

opposite: *Johnston's Canyon*, Banff National Park, Stephen Hutchings

opposite: *Maligne Lake*, Jasper National Park, Carole Harmon

Ducks on Pyramid Lake, Jasper National Park, Carole Harmon

overleaf: *Samson Peak and Maligne Lake*, Jasper National Park, Carole Harmon

Sunrise, Jasper National Park, Shin Sugino

Sunset on the Icefield Parkway, Jasper National Park, Carole Harmon

opposite: *Waterfall near Wonder Pass*, Mt. Assiniboine Provincial Park, Don Harmon

Nigel Creek, Banff National Park, Stephen Hutchings

opposite: *Athabasca Falls*, Jasper National Park, Shin Sugino

Mt. Rundle, Banff National Park, Carole Harmon

Mt. Temple seen from Paradise Valley, Banff National Park, Carole Harmon.